JOHN HARBISON

FOUR SONGS OF SOLITUDE

for Solo Violin

AMP-8069

First printing: October, 1994

Associated Music Publishers, Inc.

DISTRIBUTED BY

7777 W. BLUEMOUND RD. P.O. BOX 13819 MILWAUKEE, WI 53213

Program Note

Four Songs of Solitude was composed during the summer of 1985 as a present for my wife, Rose Mary, who gave the first performance the following winter.

They are songs, not sonatas or fugues.

The first song often returns to its initial idea, always to go a different way; the constant lyrical outward flow is balanced by a refrain line that occurs twice.

The second song begins with a folksong-like melody, which is immediately answered by a more athletic idea in a key a half step higher. The dialogue between these ideas eventually fuses them together.

The most intense piece is the third song, its melody carrying large intervals and leading toward increasingly brief and intimate reflections upon itself.

The last song is the most virtuosic and intricate. Starting from a slow emblem, which is often restated, it begins a dance with an obstinate lower voice as accompaniment. This cycles out of control twice, but manages a fragile reconciliation at the end.

The solitude is the composer's, but even more the performer's. The player's world is like that of the long distance runner, especially in challenging pieces like these, and I wanted our conversation in those hours of preparation to contain subjects of equal interest to both. The listeners can, if they wish, add in their own inner distances.

—JOHN HARBISON

duration: ca. 15 minutes

premiere performance: December 11, 1985, Harvard University, Rose Mary Harbison, violin

recording: New World Records CD 80391–2, Michelle Makarski, violin

FOUR SONGS OF SOLITUDE

I.

John Harbison

II.

III.

IV.

poco accel.

Furioso

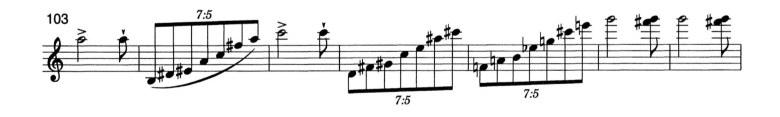

7:5

rit.

Tempo I (poco meno)

Sempre tempo I   *poco accel.*

Tempo I (poco meno)

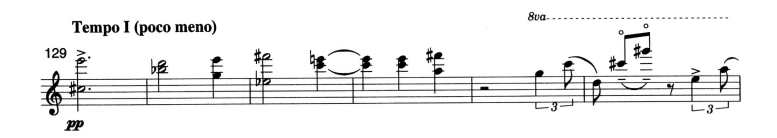